YOUR KNOWLEDGE HAS VALUE

- We will publish your bachelor's and master's thesis, essays and papers

- Your own eBook and book - sold worldwide in all relevant shops

- Earn money with each sale

Upload your text at www.GRIN.com and publish for free

Bibliographic information published by the German National Library:

The German National Library lists this publication in the National Bibliography; detailed bibliographic data are available on the Internet at http://dnb.dnb.de .

This book is copyright material and must not be copied, reproduced, transferred, distributed, leased, licensed or publicly performed or used in any way except as specifically permitted in writing by the publishers, as allowed under the terms and conditions under which it was purchased or as strictly permitted by applicable copyright law. Any unauthorized distribution or use of this text may be a direct infringement of the author s and publisher s rights and those responsible may be liable in law accordingly.

Imprint:

Copyright © 2016 GRIN Verlag
Print and binding: Books on Demand GmbH, Norderstedt Germany
ISBN: 9783668953796

This book at GRIN:

https://www.grin.com/document/470308

Alfredo Lopez

The Current Situation of Colombian Refugees in the World

A Literature Review on Existing Research

GRIN Verlag

GRIN - Your knowledge has value

Since its foundation in 1998, GRIN has specialized in publishing academic texts by students, college teachers and other academics as e-book and printed book. The website www.grin.com is an ideal platform for presenting term papers, final papers, scientific essays, dissertations and specialist books.

Visit us on the internet:

http://www.grin.com/

http://www.facebook.com/grincom

http://www.twitter.com/grin_com

The current situation of Colombian refugees in the world

By

Alfredo Lopez

2016

Table of contents

Introduction 1

The situation of displaced people before escaping from Colombia 3

The situation of Colombian refugees after escaping from Colombia 5

The situation of Colombian refugees in developing countries 6

The situation of Colombian refugees in industrialized countries 8

Conclusion 10

References 11

The current situation of Colombian refugees in the world

Introduction

Previous qualitative and quantitative research about the armed conflict in Colombia between government army forces, paramilitaries and guerrilla groups have been conducted globally (Dongen, 2005; Tobar Torres, 2015; Gottwald, 2004; Bermudez, 2013; Schussler, 2009; Shedlin, et al., 2016). According to Giraldo (2005), the armed conflict in Colombia began in 1946 and then worsened in 1960 when left-wing guerrilla groups emerged. Later, drug gangs emerged extending terror in Colombian (Gottwald, 2004). Next, in the 80s, right-wing paramilitary groups were created by rich people to combat against guerrilla forces (Giraldo, 2005). The civil war that Colombia has faced for more than 60 years has left terrible consequences in the country, part of which will be described in this literature review.

A piece of quantitative research conducted in Colombia by El Centro Nacional de Memoria Histórica de Colombia (2013) shows that 220,000 people were killed in the Colombian conflict between the years 1958-2012. Further, from that total 177,307 people were civilians and the other 40,787 were combatants in the conflict (Reyes, 2013). In addition, the research showed that from 1981 to 2012, around 150,000 people were killed in Colombia and those responsible for these deaths are as follows: Colombia's army 10.1%; guerrilla groups 16.8%; paramilitary groups 38.4%; unidentified armed groups 27.7%; other groups 7% (Reyes, 2013). The conflict in Colombia has left 1,754 victims of sexual violence from 1985-2012 (Reyes, 2013). Further, 27,023 Colombians were kidnapped between 1970 and 2010. Of these, guerrilla forces sequestered 24,482 people and 2,541 were abducted by paramilitary groups (Reyes, 2013). In addition, 25,007 Colombians are missing from 1985 to

2012. (Reyes, 2013). Another negative impact of the war in Colombia is the massive displacement of Colombians. For example, 4,744,048 Colombians were displaced from their homes from 1996 to 2012 (Reyes, 2013). During this period, there have been more than 4.7 million internally displaced, a much higher number than the population of Ireland or New Zealand (Reyes, 2013). Likewise, according to Human Rights Watch (2015), the armed conflict in Colombia has left almost six million displaced people. However, the United Nations High Commissioner for Refugee in Colombia reports that they are providing humanitarian assistance to 6,939,067 displaced people (ACNUR[1], 2015)

A large number of people displaced by violence in Colombia have felt unsafe and for that reason have escaped to neighbouring countries in search of international protection. According to ACNUR (2012) and Terra (2014), there are more than 400,000 Colombian refugees in the world. Thus, the purpose of this literature review is to provide an answer to the question: What is the current situation of the Colombian refugees in the world? Subsequently, to accomplish this objective the literature review responds to the next four sub-questions: What is the situation of displaced people before escaping from Colombia? What is the situation of Colombian refugees after escaping from Colombia? What is the situation of Colombian refugees in developing countries? And what is the situation of Colombian refugees in industrialized countries? Finally, this literature review concludes with a summary of the research and a recommendation for future research.

---

[1] Alto Comisionado de las Naciones Unidas para los Refugiados. (United Nations High Commissioner for Refugee)

The situation of displaced people before escaping from Colombia

Previous researches about displaced people in Colombia have shown the difficult situations faced by those people (Castillo, 2005). For instance, Puertas, Ríos and Del Valle (2006) explain in their quantitative and qualitative research (Mixed methodology) that a problem affecting displaced people in Colombia is mental disorders. The data collection methods used by these researchers were first, Selection of slums in Sincelejo Colombia where there is a large number of displaced persons to participate in the research (Puertas, Ríos, & del Valle, 2006). Secondly, a household survey was conducted to determine the presence of common mental disorders such as depression, anxiety and psychosomatic disorders in the population studied (Puertas, Ríos, & del Valle, 2006). Thirdly, a symptom questionnaire statement by the World Health Organization was implemented to determine the presence of a mental disorder common in people over 18 years old and to analyze this based on a mathematical and statistical score (Puertas, Ríos, & del Valle, 2006). This research concluded that a large number of people, displaced by violence, living in Sincelejo Colombia are suffering common mental disorders due to trauma caused by their forced displacements (Puertas, Ríos, & del Valle, 2006). However, it could be argued that in order to present a more reliable and credible conclusion, researchers should have used in-depth interviews, observation and focus group as data collection methods, but they did not do it that way (O'leary, 2014).

Another problem faced by internally displaced persons in Colombia is the lack of protection by the Colombian government (Carreño, 2012). For this reason, a large number of displaced people live in constant fear; in fact, many of them are persecuted by the participants of the armed conflict in Colombia (Jaramillo, Villa, & Sánchez, 2004). This situation has forced many displaced people to flee from one place to another within the country looking for safety, but even so, there have been cases where their pursuers have killed them and some other have been missing (Monroy, 2011; Jaramillo, Villa & Sánchez, 2004; Robles, 2011; Paz In Motion, 2016). These events have raised deep fears in the displaced persons and they do not feel safe to present complaints before the competent authorities of Colombia because they suspect that their persecutors infiltrate these state institutions (Riano Botina, 2012). For example, during the 90s and early 2000 many government agencies such as the police, the national army and the Attorney General's office were infiltrated by members of paramilitary groups, even right now, thousands of Columbians believe that the former president of Colombia, Alvaro Uribe Velez was a promoter and financier of paramilitary groups (Riano Botina, 2012; Morris, 2011).

Clearly, if a displaced person came to the government's agencies to denounce these armed groups, the displaced was in danger of being betrayed by these government agencies and could eventually be killed by paramilitary groups for being considered a whistle blower (Riano Botina, 2012; Morris, 2011). Consequently, thousands of displaced Colombians do not feel safe in Colombia and have preferred to cross borders to seek international protection in neighbouring countries such as Ecuador, Venezuela, Peru, Panama and Costa Rica (Gottwald, 2004). The evidence demonstrates that displaced people in Colombia are living in extremely dangerous situations before escaping from that country. Likewise, the social-economic situation of Colombian refugees after escaping from Colombia is extremely difficult.

The situation of Colombian refugees after escaping from Colombia

According to Jaramillo, Villa and Sanchez (2004), 64% of the Colombians displaced to neighbouring countries escape from death threats made by armed groups. Once they cross borders, these people are no longer internally displaced and become asylum seekers in the new country (ACNUR, 2015). However, many displaced people do not know that they have a right to apply for refugee status when arriving in another country, so they do not make a formal request for the refugee status (ACNUR, 2015). For instance, according to Jaramillo (2008) around 500,000 Colombians live in an irregular status in Ecuador, either because of ignorance of international law or simply due to fear of being rejected as refugees and consequently be deported to Colombia. Another reason that prevents Colombians from formally submitting their application for refugee status is that they believe that their pursuers could come into Ecuador looking for them; to achieve these objective criminals impersonate refugees with the purpose of finding them and kill them (Gottwald, 2004). This fear makes refuges stay undercover without the protection of the Ecuadorian government and [2]UNHCR (Gottwald, 2004). The problem already described creates other problems for these people, such as poverty and hunger (Shedlin, et al., 2016).

Many Colombian refugees have felt forced to escape quickly from Colombia abandoning their belongings, so the clothes they were wearing were all they owned for starting a new life in a different country (Paz In Motion, 2016). This shows the state of poverty of Colombian refugees arriving in a new country. Thus, in these deplorable conditions, the newcomers begin noticing that it is very hard to be out of Colombia because they have to deal with poverty, which makes it more difficult integrating into the community (Kniffki & Reutlinger, 2016). Under these conditions' poverty, refugees lack the

---

[2] United Nations High Commissioner for Refugee

most basic food and many of them feel miserable about having to come to a foreign country in search of protection (Shedlin, et al., 2016). It is obviously true that the situation of refugees after escaping from Colombia to move into underdeveloped countries is traumatic and challenging for them (Gottwald, 2004). In these countries, the Colombian refugees are suffering from many problems, some of which are described below.

The situation of Colombian refugees in developing countries

Generally, Colombians escaping from their country searching international protection arriving in developing countries such as Ecuador, Venezuela, Panama, Peru, Brazil and Costa Rica (Gottwald, 2004). When Colombians come to these countries they hope to find peace and security that Colombia does not provide, but unfortunately, this is not the case because they start experiencing problems that remove their mental peace and quietness (Shedlin, et al., 2016).

One of the main issues that Colombian refugees have to face is discrimination (Schussler, 2009). For instance, anywhere in Ecuador Colombians are discriminated against (Shedlin, et al., 2016; Schussler, 2009; Gottwals, 2004). To most Ecuadorians, Colombian men are criminals, drug traffickers, guerrillas or members of paramilitary groups (Shedlin, et al., 2016; Schussler, 2009; Gottwals, 2004). Likewise, Ecuadorians usually think that Colombian women are prostitutes and lovers of criminals (Shedlin, et al., 2016). Discrimination against Colombians in that country is so enormous that many employers do not offer jobs to them due to a common belief that Colombians are dishonest and unreliable (Shedlin, et al., 2016). In addition, the vast majority of Colombians find it arduous to get a place to live in Ecuador because Ecuadorians deny renting to Colombian refugees (Ayala,

2004). Furthermore, some stores refuse to sell their products to Colombian refugees (Shedlin, et al., 2016). These discriminating situations faced by Colombian refugees in Ecuador and in other developing countries impede find decent and stable employment (Gottwald, 2004).

Qualitative research conducted by Shedlin et al. (2016) shows that food insecurity is another issue that Colombian refugees have to face in developing countries. A study implemented in Ecuador during two years using qualitative methods such as in-depth interviews with refugees, focus groups and interviews with key informants, showed that food insecurity is the greatest issue faced by the Colombian refugees in Ecuador (Shedlin, et al., 2016). Although this study showed poor dietary conditions for Colombian refugees in Ecuador, it did not disclose approximate statistics regarding those suffering specifically from that problem. However, it is believed that almost every refugee is suffering from the same food insecurity issue in Ecuador and in all developing countries (Gottwald, 2004). To illustrate this fact a Colombian refugee in Ecuador states:

> Well, my kids sometimes, sometimes did not eat enough, many times I went without eating...because I didn't have money, I didn't have a stable job, I didn't have access. Well, it's different when you're home [in Colombia], you go to your mom, even though you disguise it, 'Hi mom, how're you doing this morning?' And then they offer you lunch, [you can go to] your sister, [or] a friend. Here it's not like that, or it could be that we don't have family here and we don't have a close friend with whom you can pretend you don't know anything at lunchtime, and help wash the dishes so they feed you; there wasn't a way, so we endured [the hunger]. (Shedlin, et al, 2016, p. 44)

We can conclude, therefore, that the situation of Colombian refugees in Ecuador and in developing countries is extremely difficult to handle. Contrastingly, the current situation of Colombian refugees in industrialized countries seems to be better.

The situation of Colombian refugees in industrialized countries

According to Arsenault (2010), Osorio and Orjuela (2009) the social-economic situation of the Colombian refugees in **Quebec Canada** is better than the current situation of the Colombian refugees in developing countries. For example, in 2005, 35,768 Colombians were welcomed as refugees in Canada and all of them received satisfactory support from the government to rebuild their lives in this industrialized country (Arsenault, 2010). The social aid that Colombian refugees have received in Canada from the government and non-government agencies have allowed them to send money regularly to their families in Colombia (Osorio & Orjuela, 2009). The above-described situation is not possible for Colombian refugees living in developing countries such as Ecuador, where many refugee women have to become a prostitute to get money to eat (Gárate, 2014).

Likewise, qualitative fieldwork research conducted by Bermudez (2013) in the **United Kingdom** between 2003 and 2007 about the experiences of Colombian refugees living in London showed that their socio-economic situation is decent. Nevertheless, integration for Colombian refugees in London has not been easy. For instance, many Colombian refugees in the United Kingdom have struggled to learn the English language, this, in turn, prevents them from have socio-economic integration (Bermudez, 2013). Although integration of Colombian refugees in the United Kingdom has not been easy, their socio-economic situation is much better than experienced by refugees in underdeveloped countries where refugees have to face food insecurity issues (Bermudez, 2013; Shedlin, et al.,2016).

Similarly, the lifestyle and situation of Colombian refugees and migrants in the United States of America is much better than the conditions Colombian refugees in developing countries (MPI, 2015). For example, concerning Colombians' lifestyle in South Florida Gollier and Gamarra (2003), affirm:

> Colombians can move to South Florida and feel safe while not substantially changing their lifestyles. A plethora of Colombian products are available in South Florida supermarkets. The number of Colombian restaurants in the region is increasing. South Florida cultural activities (music, dance, arts, etc.) are similar to those in Colombia. Colombian radio networks and TV programs are readily available on South Florida Spanish-language stations. Colombian newspapers and magazines are also available in South Florida or can be read easily on the Internet. These factors, combined with the dominant Spanish language and existing social networks of family and friends, allow Colombians to live almost identical lives to the way they did in their home state (minus the security threats). (p. 5)

The evidence demonstrates that the situation of Colombian refugees in industrialized countries is better than the situation of them in developing countries. However, in any country where Colombian refugees are, they miss their country of origin and at some point, they are affected by Ulysses syndrome, which is a series of symptoms caused by excess stress that affects to immigrants and refugees. Normally, Ulysses syndrome affects immigrants' adaptation (Delgado, 2008).

Conclusion

In summary, this literature review has described the current situation of Colombian refugee in the world by responding to the question: what is the current situation of the Colombian refugees in the world? Firstly, the review has shown the dangerous situation of displaced people before escaping from Colombia. Secondly, the literature review has described the terrible situation faced by Colombian refugees after escaping from Colombia. Thirdly, the situation of Colombian refugees in developing countries was compared with the situation of Colombian refugees in industrialized countries. Therefore, this review has found that the social-economic situation of the Colombian refugee in industrialized countries is much better than the social-economic situation of Colombian refugees in developing countries. However, all of them miss Colombia their own land.

To conclude, this literature review has also described briefly the social-economic situation of Colombian refugees in countries such as Ecuador, Canada, United Kingdom, United States of America and others. But, there are not research about Colombian refugees in New Zealand and their experiences of resilience, resettlement and integration in this South Pacific country. Thus, this opens the door for future research on the topic of Colombian refugees in New Zealand and their resettlement in this country.

References

ACNUR. (2015). *Tendencias globales.* Geneva: UNHCR.

Arsenault, S. (2010). *Relations under tension: Colombian refugees in Quebec.* Bogotá Colombia: Universidad Nacional de Colombia.

Ayala, M. (2004, January 29). *Colombianos en Ecuador, entre la xenofobia y la admiración.* Retrieved from Eltiempo: http://www.eltiempo.com/archivo/documento/MAM-1533879

Bermudez, A. (2013). A gendered perspective on the arrival and settlement of Colombian refugees in the United Kingdom. *Journal of Ethnic and Migration Studies*, 39,7, 1159-1175.

Carreño, A. M. (2012). *Colombia: Consecuencias del conflicto interno, actores e instituciones.* Santigo de Chile: Revista Encrucijada Americana.

Castillo, O. L. (2005). Poblaciones en situación de desplazamiento forzado en Colombia: Una revisión de las cifras del sistema de información RUT. *Cuadernos de Desarrollo Rural*, 29-50.

Collier, M., & Gamarra, E. (2003). *The Colombian Diaspora in South Florida.* Dallas, Texas: Florida International University.

Delgado, P. (2008). Migration and psychopathology. *Anuario de psicología clínica y de la salud*, 4, 15-25.

Dongen, R. V. (2005). Colombia's Civil War: A long-running conflict in this South American nation has forced 3 million people from their homes. *Junior Scholastic*, 107(15), 14.

Elespectador. (2012, June 20). *Colombia: cuatro Millones de desplazados y 400 mil refugiados.* Retrieved from Elespectador: http://www.elpais.com.uy/informacion/pedidos-refugio-crecen-mitad-llega.html

Gárate, A. (2014). Human trafficking for sexual exploitation between Colombia and Ecuador. *Debate*, 16, 181-198.

Giraldo, J. F. (2005). Colombia armed conflict? 1946-1985. *Papel Político*, 18, 43-78.

Gottwald, M. (2004). Protecting Colombian refugees in the Andean region: The fight against. *International Journal of Refugee Law*, 16, 4, 517–546.

Human Rights Watch. (2015). *Resumen del país: Colombia.* New York: Human Rights Watch.

Jaramillo, A. M., Villa, M. I., & Sánchez, L. A. (2004). *Miedo y desplazamiento: Experiencias y percepciones.* Medellín Colombia: Corporacion Region.

Jaramillo, L. (2008). *La población colombiana irregular en el Ecuador: Hacia su regularización.* Quito Ecuador: Universidad andina Simón Bolívar.

Juan, M. C. (2011, April 16). *Desplazados: amenazados, asesinados y sin protección.* Retrieved from ElColombiano:

http://www.elcolombiano.com/historico/desplazados_amenazados_asesinados_y_si n_proteccion-JGEC_129990

Kniffki, J., & Reutlinger, C. (2016). *El trabajo social desde miradas transnacionales: Experiencias empíricas y conceptuales.* Berlin: Frank & Timme GmbH.

Morris, C. (2011, September 7). *Paramilitar vincula al expresidente Uribe en supuesta formación de grupos paramilitares.* Retrieved from Youtube: https://www.youtube.com/watch?v=ocFJE6u04vc

MPI. (2015). *The Colombian Diaspora in the United States.* Washington: Migration policy institute.

O'leary, Z. (2014). *The essential guide to doing your research project (2nd ed.).* London: SAGE.

Osorio, F. E., & Orjuela, A. (2009). En busca de progreso y protección: Experiencias de inmigrantes económicos y refugiados colombianos en Québec, Canadá. *Perspectivas Colombo-Canadienses, 2*, 30-44.

Paz In Motion. (2016, May 18). *El drama humanitario en Colombia ¿A dónde llegan los desplazados?* Retrieved from Las2Orillas: http://www.las2orillas.co/el-drama-humanitario-de-colombia-a-donde-llegan-los-desplazados/

Puertas, G., Ríos, C., & del Valle, H. (2006). Prevalencia de trastornos mentales comunes en barrios marginales urbanos. *Panam Salud Publica/Pan Am J Public Health*, 20(5):324–30.

Reyes, E. (2013, July 24). *El conflicto armado en Colombia deja 220.000 muertos desde 1958.* Retrieved from El país: http://internacional.elpais.com/internacional/2013/07/24/actualidad/1374677621_928074.html

Riano Botina, R. M. (2012, April 21). *Máxima infiltración paramilitar en Colombia*. Retrieved from youtube: https://www.youtube.com/watch?v=A1fTDmALe5Q

Robles, A. (2011, March 1). *Colombia: 250 mil desaparecidos.* Retrieved from Eldiariointernacional: http://www.eldiariointernacional.com/spip.php?article3040

Schussler, S. (2009). *Entre la sospecha y la ciudadanía: Refugiados Colombianos en Quito.* Quito, Ecuador: Ediciones Abya-Yala.

Shedlin, M., Decena, C., Noboa, H., Betancourt, O., Birdsall, S., & Smith, K. (2016). The impact of food insecurity on the health of Colombian refugees in Ecuador. *Journal of Food Security*, 4, 2, 42-51 doi: 10.12691/jfs-4-2-3.

Terra, G. (2014, January 26). *Pedidos de Refugio screen y la mitad llega de Colombia.* Retrieved from Elpaís: http://www.elpais.com.uy/informacion/pedidos-refugio-crecen-mitad-llega.html

Tobar Torres, J. A. (2015). Political violence and dirty war in Colombia. remembrance of a victim of the Colombian conflict in relation to the Havana negotiations. *Memoria Y Sociedad*, 19(38), 9-22 doi:10.11144/Javeriana.mys19-38.vpgs.

YOUR KNOWLEDGE HAS VALUE

- We will publish your bachelor's and master's thesis, essays and papers

- Your own eBook and book -
  sold worldwide in all relevant shops

- Earn money with each sale

Upload your text at www.GRIN.com
and publish for free